THE BALLOU

~~THEY SEE~~
~~THEY ASSUME~~
~~THEY JUDGE~~
~~THEY DISMISS~~

WE KNOW

Published by
Shout Mouse Press, Inc.
www.shoutmousepress.org

Copyright © 2019 Shout Mouse Press, Inc.

All rights reserved.
ISBN-13: 978-1945434914 (Shout Mouse Press, Inc.)
ISBN-10: 1945434910

Book Design by Barrett Smith

Photographs/Artwork

The lined paper texture used on pg. 41 was licensed under a Creative Commons Attribution License and created by D. Sharon Pruitt from USA

All photography produced in partnership with Lana Wong/Shootback Project

Student photography featured on pages 5, 15, 19, 21, 25, 26, 29, 33, 35, 40, 45, 49, 59, 64

DEDICATION

This book is dedicated to our truth,
and to all those bold, courageous, oustanding people we love.

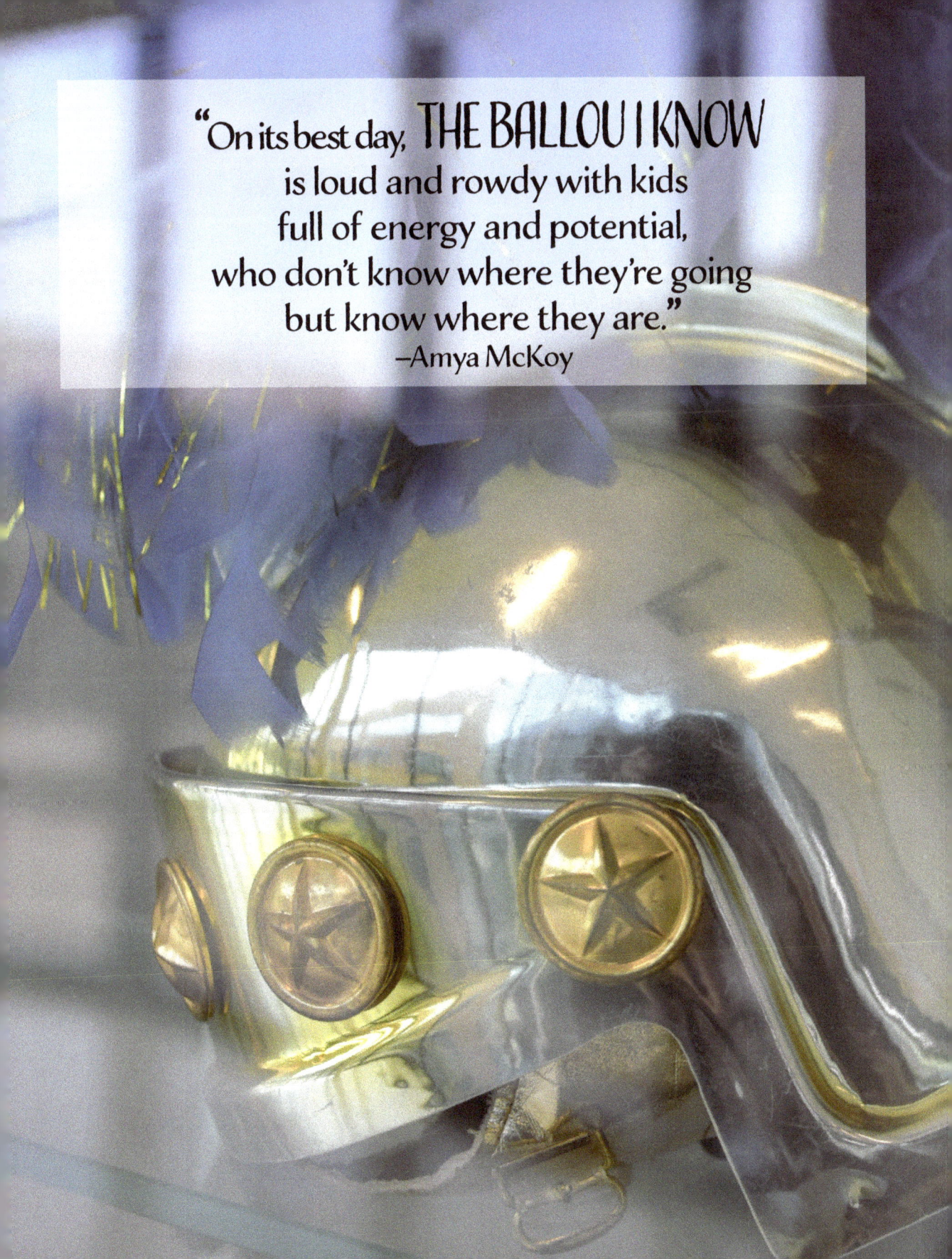

"On its best day, THE BALLOU I KNOW is loud and rowdy with kids full of energy and potential, who don't know where they're going but know where they are."
—Amya McKoy

CONTENTS

Amya McKoy & Tatiana Robinson • Introduction

Ahmaiya Pleze • Transformative — 2

Aniyah Lester • Where Do We Go? — 4

Shaheed Salim • Ma Rowe — 6

Gabriel Clark • Why I Dream Big Dreams — 8

The Ballou I Know — 11

Jada Byrd • Where Would I Be? — 12

Me'Chelle Jones • The Ballou I Know — 14

Andrenae Brown • A Letter to My Cousin — 16

The Ballou I Know — 19

Tatiana Robinson • Letter From the Future — 20

Syamyia Beach • Flipping the Script — 22

The Ballou I Know — 25

Trevaughn Boomer • Texting Our Truth — 26

Tyrese Linder • Dig Deeper — 30

The Ballou I Know — 33

Shawma Brown • A Scandalous Perception	34
Cashae Faison • College-Bound	36
The Ballou I Know	38
Tremayne Gross • If Ballou Didn't Exist	39
Darmeisha Moore • The Ballou I Know	42
Davia Cain • Looking Up	44
Amya McKoy • A Response From Truth	46
The Ballou I Know	49
Christopher Holbrook • The Ballou I Know	50
Shae'Lynn Ames • Let's Be Real	52
Raven Brown • The Ballou I Know	54
Milan Womack • The Love Inside	56
The Ballou I Know	59

Afterword

Acknowledgments

About Shout Mouse Press and Shootback

INTRODUCTION
Amya McKoy and Tatiana Robinson

June 13, 2017. The Ballou High School class of 2017 graduated, and to great acclaim. This class had achieved something amazing: every senior had applied to college. Even better, every single graduate had been accepted into at least one school. We were celebrating. We felt like this was a great accomplishment. It made the underclassmen proud and pushed us to do better. It gave the alumni a new-found pride and reminded them why their alma mater was so great. The whole community celebrated Ballou's triumph. We felt like the pride and joy of Southeast.

And it didn't stop there; the news spread nationwide. Students were interviewed on the radio and on television. There were stories in newspapers from places all over, even places we'd never heard of before. Headlines said "Entire Class Accepted Into College" and "Ballou High School Makes History." Ballou had finally been able to dig itself out of the bad stigmas that surrounded its name. We were on top of the world.

But, on November 28, 2017, not even six months later, the first article came out. It was called "What Really Happened At the School Where Every Graduate Got Into College." Our world came crashing down.

They told *their* story — a story they put together based on incomplete reporting, disgruntled employees, and what they *thought* was the truth. But it was an outsider's perspective. They only captured half the story. They already had a negative image of the Ballou they thought they knew, and that's the Ballou the world chose to believe.

We're not saying Ballou is a perfect school. We have our ups and downs, and we're rough around the edges. As the reporting showed, there are some real issues that need to be discussed. But those things don't define us. And more importantly, THEY don't define us.

We tried to tell our story before, we tried to clear our name, but to no avail. They ignored our pleas. To them we were just Southeast kids, and more specifically we were just Ballou kids. The negativity had already been stamped on our names.

This is our last line of defense. These are our stories, from our perspectives. No matter what the journalists think, we are the only ones who know "What *Really* Happened at the School Where Every Graduate Got Into College." And this book conveys our truth: the highs and the lows of the place that we call home. Because what none of those articles captured was that Ballou is our home, and we are a family.

This is The Ballou We Know.

THIS IS OUR LAST LINE OF ◄ **DEFENSE** ►

THESE ARE OUR *stories*

TRANSFORMATIVE
Ahmaiya Pleze

I'm not the person I was in middle school. Those were difficult days. I didn't care much for the students or the teachers, and I'm not sure they cared much for me. I had a bad reputation.

I was a fighter. I was always fighting and getting into trouble, and that didn't get me anywhere but out of school for a long time, just when I needed to be there.

Ballou was different.

From my first year here, Ms. Yates has been a mentor to me - talking to me, telling me about life, pushing me, staying on top of me. She cared about me, and I wanted to make her proud. My mom has always been there for me too, but when someone outside of your home, someone outside of your family, takes an interest like that, it really means something.

It hasn't all been easy here. In tenth grade, I started fighting again, and got suspended, for a long time. But this time, I started to realize it wasn't worth it. I started to realize that I could control how I react to things. I can choose to walk away instead of fighting. I was determined to do better, and Ms. Yates helped me gain the confidence I needed to do it.

I don't fight anymore. I used to give up on my schoolwork, but I don't give up anymore. I get As and Bs now in AP English and Honors Math.

I'm looking ahead now. I want to go to college to study criminal justice, and eventually forensic science. Someday, I'd like to own my own business. If you asked my closest friends about me today, they would say, "If she wants to get it done, she'll get it done."

I'm not the person I was in middle school. Now that I am in an environment where my teachers care about me, I look back and realize that's what I needed then. I didn't have a lot of support from my middle school teachers to prepare me for the real world and high school. But I do have that at Ballou.

My experience here has been great. And because of it, I have a better work ethic, better communication skills, and less drama. I learned that I must take things seriously, especially school.

There's a lot of negative criticism of Ballou on social media and in the news. But those people don't know Ballou or us. That criticism has only made us become closer and has made us want to speak up. They don't talk about how transformative Ballou can be.

I'm not the person I was in middle school.
I'm a better student and a more mature person.

That happened at Ballou.

"I'M NOT THE PERSON I WAS IN MIDDLE SCHOOL..."

AHMAIYA PLEZE
I'm from Washington, DC. I wrote this to tell my story. In the future, I want to become a forensic scientist and give back to my community. I enjoy doing great things for myself and influencing others.

WHERE DO WE GO?
Aniyah Lester

I wake up, I wake my daughter up. I get us dressed and then we're on our way to Ballou.

Every day, my mother drops us off at school. When we arrive I go to the daycare downstairs and I say, "Bye, bye, MeMe," and give my baby a hug and a kiss. She used to cry when I left but now she knows I'm coming back. She's being a big girl now. She'll be two in June and I'm sad because she's growing up so fast.

If there was no Ballou, I would wake up and think, "Where do we go?" If I just stayed in the house, my daughter would not have the opportunity to grow into a big girl like this. She would not be learning to be independent.

Instead, I drop her off at Ballou's daycare and I'm off to class. I put my stuff in my locker and get ready to learn. Like my daughter, I learn something new every day — especially in math class. I know math is going to help me in the future, because I want to own my own business. I don't know what kind yet, but because of Ballou, I'll be ready.

There could be no Ballou to go to, and I wouldn't know what was possible. I wouldn't even have the idea to open my own business. I could end up with a regular job, like at McDonald's (not that there's anything wrong with that), but I want to do something different from what people expect. I don't want to be a statistic.

> "I WANT TO DO SOMETHING DIFFERENT FROM WHAT PEOPLE EXPECT. I DON'T WANT TO BE A STATISTIC."

At Ballou I have a support group. It's called New Heights. People from all over, like colleges and Children's Hospital, come to talk to us. They give us advice and resources.

Without Ballou, I wouldn't have a support group. It would be just me and my mother. My mother is great but it helps to have people around who have been in my shoes. It helps me because they're more understanding of where I'm coming from and what it's like to be a teen mom.

I am so grateful that I'm a Knight. At Ballou, I know my life is meaningful, because I get another chance to become somebody that I want to be.

ANIYAH LESTER
I'm from Maryland, but I grew up in Southeast. I wrote this because I wanted to share my true story my own way. In the future I want to own my own clothing business and become a motivational speaker. I enjoy working and learning new things. My hobbies are shopping and giving advice. I want people to know that I'm a go-getter and don't stop.

MA ROWE
Shaheed Salim

If I didn't have my counselor, Ms. Rowe, I think my high school experience would have looked a lot different. In a bad way. I wouldn't be in the position I am today to pursue my dreams.

When I first met Ms. Rowe, I actually thought she was mean. She always had a serious look on her face, and the way she carried herself was like she didn't play no games. At first I was nervous to talk to her, like I sometimes am with new people. And since I was new to high school, I didn't know who I could trust. My middle school friends had told me that in high school the teachers don't care about you. They won't help. So coming into high school, that's what I thought.

But one day at the beginning of high school I was in my class and Ms. Rowe walked in and asked for me to step out in the hallway. Then I was confused. What did I have to step in the hallway for? I knew I didn't do nothing wrong; I was just doing what I was supposed to do. But she introduced herself to me as my counselor, and said she wanted to get to know me better. When we were talking, I found out that she was actually nice and caring. And then after that, I thought I should give her a chance. She might help me through high school.

And she did.

From then on, I would go to Ms. Rowe's office almost every day to check on my grades and make sure I was on track to pass. I knew she had something to offer, some knowledge she could give me for the future. She just wanted the best for me. She wanted me to be different, not like everybody else. She didn't want me to fall into the wrong crowd. She would give me advice like, "Hang out with people who have the same goals as you," or "Your ninth grade year is your most important year because your grades from here can help you in the long run." I wanted to be successful, so I listened to her advice and I did my best. Our bond has gotten so close that I call her 'Ma Rowe' now.

I never thought I could manage a 3.5 GPA throughout all my high school years, but as a senior, I've been successful at managing that goal. I've won the Male Student Athlete Award, made honor roll every quarter, and learned to focus on all my classes.

My success has been a combination of my relationship with Ms. Rowe, and with other teachers, too, like Ms. Ingram and Ms. Yates. It turned out my middle school friends were wrong — the teachers here at Ballou High School DID care. If I asked for help, they were always there. If I asked a question, they would take time to answer. If I didn't understand what was going on in the class, I would stay after school, and they would help. In general they would always communicate with me and tell me what I needed to work on in order to get better. My teachers motivated me to do better in school and influenced me to go to college. They helped me take initiative in my own learning so I could be successful.

My success is due to a lot of people, but it's also because of something deep within me. I've had to work very hard to be where I am, and I have to balance a lot. I've got school, I've got sports, and I've got homework. That means after a three-hour practice I still have to go home and finish my homework. Having to balance my time is tiring, but it's also making me better as a man. And it shows that I can handle responsibility for my future.

I've grown so much since I was that boy in the hallway meeting Ms. Rowe. I will graduate soon, and I have plans. I want to be a college athlete and major in mathematics, then go on to get my master's degree. I want to be able to provide for my family in the future. I know I can do it. My time at Ballou taught me how: just stay focused and put my mind to it.

SHAHEED SALIM

I'm from Washington, DC. I wrote this because I want everybody to hear our point of view of what Ballou is like. In the future, I want to go to a four year university and play college football and major in math. I enjoy playing video games and football and reading. I want people to know that I'm hard working and outgoing.

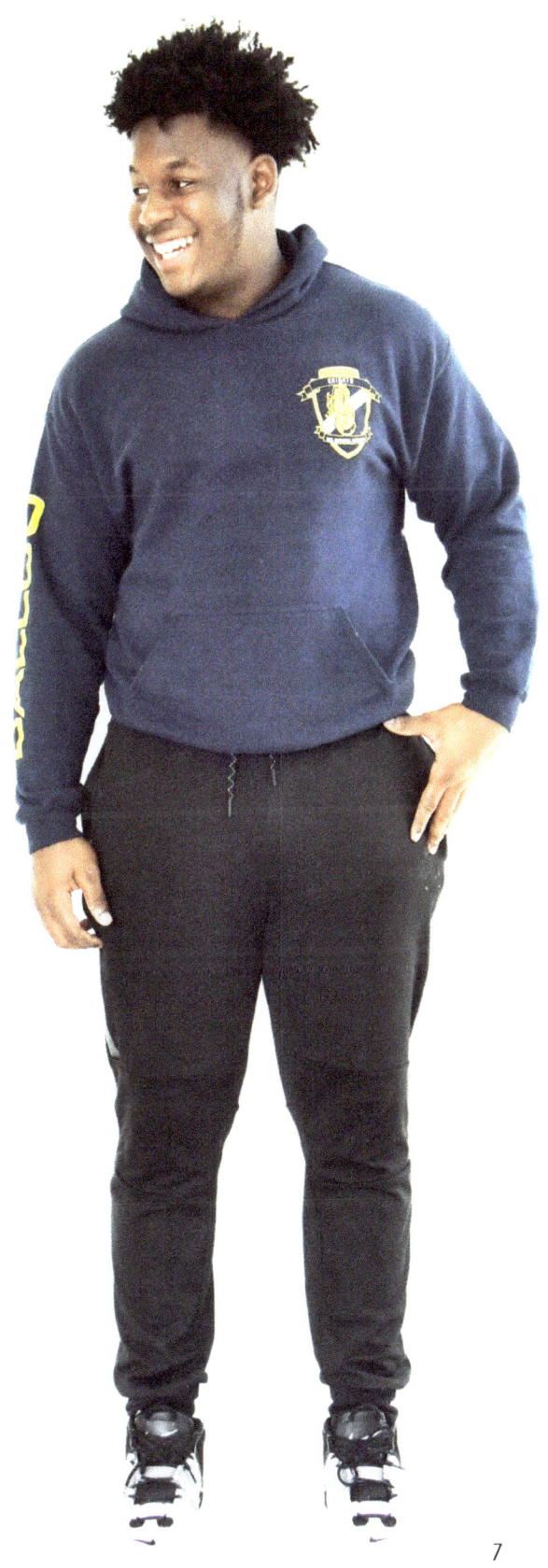

WHY I DREAM BIG DREAMS: A SELF-INTERVIEW
Gabriel Clark

Hey. Can I ask a question? It might sound kinda ...
Sure...

How do you do it?
Do what?

Like, keep positive. Keep focused.
I dream big dreams. I know it's not just about me.

What do you mean?
I mean there are younger people with dreams like mine. If I can achieve my goals, I prove to them that it's possible.

It's hard, though, right?
I mean, yeah. I'm faced with so much adversity. It's a basic ghetto adversity, you know, being less privileged. You're put at a disadvantage. Family problems, money problems. Violence. It becomes like the norm, like our reality. Certain things don't faze us the way they would faze other people. If there were gunshots around, we wouldn't scatter and be worried. That's our normal environment.

I feel you. It's messed up.
Yeah. Also, you know the type of education in the areas where we grow up? There's a lack of resources in our schools compared to other schools. We're put behind the eight-ball. It's harder to maneuver towards success.

Yeah. Some days I just wanna give up, you know?
Sure. But failure is not an option. My failure means I've let down the future generations to come. My failure means my siblings have no one to look up to. Why? Because my family is expecting me to make it out. And I'm going to get out, by any means necessary.

Seems like your family really motivates you.
Talking about my family brings a clash of different characters, different emotions. Family is complicated, right? The thing is, I've made a lot of mistakes that I'm not very proud of. I don't want my siblings to make those same mistakes. I don't want them to have an obstructed view of what it takes to be successful. I don't want them to feel like they are without right now, or that they'll be without forever.

That's deep. Did you used to think you'd always be without?
Yeah maybe. I used to think that not much was possible. I didn't have college dreams. I didn't know that focusing on schoolwork could take you anywhere. I didn't think I could reach my goals.

What changed?
It started when I moved in with my father. He gave me an ultimatum one day on the football field. He gave me two choices. He could be very blunt. He was like, "Either go out there

"MY DREAMS CAN SHINE A LIGHT UPON THE DARKNESS, CAN EASE THE OVERLY OPPRESSED."

GABRIEL CLARK

I'm from Maryland. I wrote this because I wanted to share what it's like for the students at Ballou. In the future, I want to give back to the youth. My hobbies are working out and writing. I want people to see my ambition.

and play football, or I'm gonna put my foot up your butt." So you know what I did.

I started to realize that I had talent, and if I wanted to further that talent, I was going to have to work on school.

He sounds like a good father.
Yeah, my father shined a light on ways that I could succeed. He put things in place so I could focus more on schoolwork. He made me believe that change could also be a good thing. Growing up, 'change' never really had a positive meaning. It normally meant something was being taken away or I had to leave something or someone. But I started to learn that change could open doors. When you truly want to be successful you have to be willing to change yourself.

So where are you now, like on your path to success?
Right now I'm in a position where I'm able to go to college for free. I'm a 3.0 student. Yesterday, I committed to go to Morgan State and be a student athlete. I'm starting to come to peace with a lot of things, letting go of built-up emotion so I can be calmer. Now, the sky is the limit. No one can tell me what I'm not going to be anymore.

That's dope. You should be proud. Do you think your "big dreams" helped get you here?
Tupac once said, "Reality is wrong, dreams are for real." I believe that. My reality was wrong, but my dreams are for real. And my dreams will change the way that all those around me dream. Being young still puts me in the race to make change, to create yellow brick roads for those who are lost. My dreams can shine a light upon the darkness, can ease the overly oppressed. Like Wale said: "Dream big and follow through even bigger."

Last question is hard. What if you don't succeed?
If I don't succeed? I don't even ask myself that. Failure is not an option.

I know it goes against what I've been told, but I have no time to work on a plan B because I'm too focused on plan A. I have to go to college. I have to be successful. I have to recreate the narrative for young black students in America.

My father doesn't work long hours and lose sleep just for me to be mediocre. God doesn't continuously bless me just for me to be average.

But I don't count on others to tell me if I've made it or not. To me, success is a state of mind. When a person reaches their needs to be happy, then they are successful. I created a way for me to be able to go to college without my parents having to pay a whole bunch of money. I'm going to work with kids because I want to help people, at a young age, so they don't become broken adults. I will feel successful if I can spark something in the mind of someone who will change the world.

"THE BALLOU I KNOW is loud and hard and soft and always alive. It's a homecoming of emotions and morals and troubles."

– Amya McKoy

WHERE I BELONG
Jada Byrd

When I first came to Ballou I had nothing but negative thoughts on this school. I thought I would change for the worse. I believed that I would just be stuck in the same position of constantly repeating the things I was trying to overcome and let go of. When I say that I mean the pain, the hardships, the distractions, and the reality of what it's like for a young black girl living in Southeast, or the "hood." I wanted to change my attitude and my mindset, so I needed to feel good about where I was going, and at the time it just wasn't Ballou.

I had already gotten expelled from Thurgood Marshall Academy for fighting. I had all this anger inside of me. I believed that as soon as someone said something I didn't like then I had to fight. But I didn't want to act that way anymore. I really wanted to change. I set goals for myself to be a better person, and I looked forward to a fresh start.

When the time came for me to start school again my mother wanted me to stay somewhere close to home because of the violence in Southeast. I tried another school first, but it didn't work for me. Within a few weeks, I ended up at Ballou.

The very first day I walked into Ballou, I didn't want to be there. This wasn't where I saw myself. I judged Ballou based on things I'd heard, and I was afraid I wouldn't be able to change there. But soon after, my mind completely changed.

> "I KNEW I BELONGED HERE WHEN I MET GIRLS WHO WERE TRYING TO BECOME BETTER."

It all started when I met two girls named Nadia and Raven. These girls were cool and I was interested in learning more about them. I wanted them to tell me more about the school. They were the ones who helped me get around and meet even more people. I felt like myself when I was around them, and that is the most important thing to feel when going to a new environment and being around new people. So from that day forward I was fine with the school and the people in it. Of course I wasn't friends with everyone and that's just life, but I felt welcomed and safe at Ballou and that feeling is very meaningful. A week into school, I realized that it was good for me to be here.

The next year, in tenth grade, we went on an all-girls retreat. We all went to a cabin. We were in groups. We did a lot of hiking, obstacle courses, camping, etc. We were getting to know each other more every single day and it was needed and very helpful. At some point, we were all sharing our feelings and personal experiences. It was life-changing to know that there was more

to life than my problems, even though they sometimes felt overwhelming. I knew I could be selfish when it came to things like that. I always felt like nobody knew who I was and what I'd been through. But at that retreat I learned that there were people who had been through things far worse than I had.

I knew I belonged here when I met girls who were trying to become better. It was like we were trying to cover up something. We were all opening up but not all the way. We were still trying to hide something without realizing that it would help us all to just let it all out. We knew each other, but we still felt as though we couldn't tell each other everything because we didn't know how long friendships would last, and if they were ever even real enough to hold on to.

We were — and still are — learning and growing as a school and as teenagers, period. We started to connect with one another deeper than we all believed we would. I started to feel like I wanted to stay at this school and that this is where I belong. So now I am a senior and cannot wait to graduate with the class of 2K19. Even though I am still a little sad that it is all about to come to an end, this journey has been life-changing and I am blessed to have shared it with my peers at school. I AM BOLD, COURAGEOUS, and OUTSTANDING. I am Ballou.

JADA BYRD

I'm from Washington, DC. I wrote this to further explain the real Ballou. In the future I want to become a successful criminal lawyer. I enjoy social media, writing music, and singing. I want people to know that I am just a young black girl learning her way. Before you judge someone or something, check the reality of your life and the lives around you.

THE BALLOU I KNOW
Me'Chelle Jones

ME'CHELLE JONES
I wrote this to show that Ballou students are powerful and bright enough to determine their own future. In the future I want to be a counselor to give back to kids like Ballou students. I enjoy helping people and expressing myself. My hobby is cheering. I want people to know that I am strong, determined, and love myself.

THE BALLOU I KNOW is a place to call home
And the opening between that rock and a hard place
It's a step ladder to my success
It is teaching young adults how to grow
and empower each other
On its best day,
the Ballou I know is a paradise and an empire
On tough days,
it's the same as all other places
You might not know from the outside looking in,
Or from looking away,
Or from not looking at all,
But the Ballou I know is a home
that gives everyone a chance

A LETTER TO MY COUSIN:
FOR HIS FIRST DAY OF HIGH SCHOOL
Andrenae Brown

Dear Cousin,

High school for me has been fun, but it has also been a rocky road. Before you get started, I would like to send you some advice.

I know that middle school may have seemed easy and relaxed, but now that you're entering high school it's going to be a whole different ball game. You will see yourself changing and maturing. Sometimes you will have difficulties, and you will find yourself in challenging positions. You will have moments where you feel stuck, whether it's with work or with personal situations. But I'm going to give you some tips on how to stick it out and get through whatever issues you may have.

- **Don't get caught up in what others want you to be.**

People always tell me that I should be a model. They tell me I'm tall, I'm slim. They think I look like what a model should be. But I don't want to be a model. I want to be an entrepreneur. I want to own my own business. I want to be my own boss. So I join programs to learn how to build my vision, and I take classes like AVID to prepare me for college. If I only listened to what others said, it would defeat my purpose of being happy. That's what I want for you. Always follow what YOU want to do, what you want to be. Let no one tell you otherwise.

> "PUT YOUR BEST FOOT FORWARD, AND KEEP WALKING TOWARDS YOUR VISION."

- **Prepare for the best AND the worst.**

You can handle the educational stuff, but your mind isn't prepared for high school if things are distracting you from being in the moment. I should know.

The end of my ninth-grade year, my mom got shot. One day she was picking me up from my sister's house and we were standing outside talking when all of a sudden people started shooting. We were the only people out there. We were four girls... It's hard to think about, even today.

I tried not to let the event replay or linger too deeply in my thoughts. Still, living a fun high school experience was hard throughout this time. Instead of going to football games I was going home and taking care of my mother. But for me the key was staying focused on school more than my personal life to keep my mind off what happened. With time, I grew to let this obstacle be my motivation, and I pushed myself beyond what even I knew that I could do.

With this being said, I want you to push through any obstacles you may come across throughout high school. Never let anything prevent you from fulfilling your dreams. I know you can do it because I have done it and am still continuing to do it. I'm here to support you, whatever comes.

- Be the change you want to see in the world.

Look for ways to find where you belong, and it may not be in school. I found my standing through my church, where my aunt took me to conferences every year. One year, we did a service trip. We went somewhere in Philly and helped clean up the neighborhood and did activities with other youth. Doing that inspired me to want to be the lead for my group and represent where I come from. So that year I ran for President of the International Council of Community Churches, and I won. Now going on my third year, I have been influencing other youth who may want to be in my position one day. I am giving them the courage and opportunity to branch out and be something big. I want them, as well as you, to be life-changing.

Just put your best foot forward, and keep walking towards your vision. I believe that with everything, you have to have faith, and I have that in you.

I want these tips to help you along the way, and be an influence to you as you follow your given path. I will always be here, no matter how far away I am, to motivate, encourage, and support you to be your best self.

Love,

ANDRENAE BROWN

I'm a senior at Ballou from Washington, DC. I like to write, cook, and plan events. I want to be an entrepreneur and possibly open up my own restaurant. I'd also like to start a mentoring organization that mentors up-and-coming chefs. I wanted to be part of this book to get my opinion out about all the changes happening at Ballou. I want readers to see the different personalities of the students at Ballou and not to focus on the stereotypical things that people hear. Being a part of this book helped me learn to open up more and to let people hear my point of view. It allows people to get to know more about me as a person.

"THE BALLOU I KNOW is that Southeast school that people THINK they know about..."
– Andrenae Brown

#DCPSGoesToCollege

I AM BALLOU!

LETTER FROM THE FUTURE
Tatiana Robinson

Dear 16-Year-Old Tatiana,

Remember when you first accepted the position to be on the State Board of Education? And when you went to Harvard for the summer? And when you dually-enrolled in college classes? And when you played 1000 and 1 sports and were in 1000 and 1 clubs?

You stayed up late. You took challenging courses. You were stressed out and had 1000 and 1 assignments. You were tired but you kept pushing. Your family kept you motivated. You had so many people on your side, rooting for you.

Remember when they told you to be strong and keep pushing? Remember when they told you your hard work would pay off in the end? Remember when people said they could see you as mayor? And even as President?

Well, all that hard work finally paid off even though you thought it wouldn't. I thought getting the two Bachelor's in computer science and mathematics was the biggest thing, but it was just the beginning.

I started a mentoring program because when I was in Ballou Ladies of Excellence, I decided that I wanted to give back, the way people gave to me. The program is for the girls of DC and it is focused on S.T.E.M. I am somebody that they can talk to about anything. I want to be somebody they can trust. I am never too busy to help them with homework. I take them to the movies and out to eat and on field trips to wherever they want to go. I look at them and I see the younger me; they remind me of you.

I see a lot of jobs that are available in this field. I want to show young girls that S.T.E.M. is exciting, and something to be really interested in. I think it's important that we show young people that technology is the future.

Now that I am older, I realize that it is you — my younger self — who has inspired me to be great, to keep pushing, to be optimistic, and to give people what was given to me. I appreciate all my experiences, especially from high school, because these experiences taught me skills that I still use, even today.

I am a computer scientist now, and I have my doctorate degree. These days I am developing software and working at a big company that helps others. Eventually, I want to give back to my community and become mayor of DC. I am just so grateful for the ups, the downs, the accomplishments, and the setbacks. I have finally achieved my goal, and I have you to thank for it.

— *Dr. Tatiana Robinson*

"YOU HAVE INSPIRED ME
TO BE GREAT,
TO KEEP PUSHING,
TO BE OPTIMISTIC,
AND TO GIVE PEOPLE
WHAT WAS GIVEN TO ME."

TATIANA ROBINSON

I'm from Southeast, DC. I wrote this to express to younger kids that if you continue to push, hard work will pay off. In the future I want to become a computer scientist. I enjoy anything that has to do with S.T.E.M, especially coding. My hobbies are playing golf and basketball and spending time with my family. I want people to know that I am strong, independent, inquisitive, and eager to achieve my best. I am passionate about learning and am excited to attend college.

"LIKE ALL THE STUDENTS WHO MUST FIGHT FOR AN EDUCATION, THAT WORD 'AVERAGE' IS NON-EXISTENT IN OUR VOCABULARY."

FLIPPING THE SCRIPT
Syamyia Beach

This piece was sparked by reading news articles and responding to the allegations against Ballou. This was my chance to tell you the inside student view.

The school chancellor said, "I am deeply disappointed…

But I am deeply disappointed…
That social media is trying to break down the family
That family being Ballou
It's not just a school, it's a home
False allegations that kids aren't smart
That they are just handing kids degrees

In life nothing is handed to you
You have to fight for what you believe
I believe that I can be better than what society thinks of me
And that's why I strive for straight As, and I get them
But remember:
Everybody has a different story

My story is
I'm just a kid who wants to be successful
I strive for success and that's what makes me achieve
I'm not average, I'm above-
Like all the students who must fight for an education
That word 'average' is nonexistent in our vocabulary

So I am deeply disappointed
That every time we have a breakthrough
We are targeted, like a piece of meat
You don't know
You don't go here
So you don't know the truth

You don't know what's behind the glass doors
You don't get to witness the fact that
We are children being children
So of course we should expect
That we will take some wrong turns
And when society's constantly trying
To investigate our success?
You tend to lose that mustard seed of faith

My seed is staying strong
I want to look forward to the future
And not the past
I want to focus on what CAN be done
And not what HAS BEEN done
So I want to say to you…

It's about what you CAN do
It is about overcoming the things
You once thought you couldn't
Every child has trials
Every child worries
About what they have to do
Just to show up at school
And yet HERE WE ARE
We try our best

We can do anything
but we have to put our minds to it
We have to have the courage
To act without fear of the unknown
And when we do, we will see
The light at the end of the tunnel
And when we do, we will show the world
That we can go beyond
That we are no disappointment
That we are deeply committed
To success

SYAMYIA BEACH
I'm from Southeast DC. I wrote this poem because I wanted to show the people of the DMV area that DC students can overcome the obstacles that they face and the daggers that are thrown at them. In the future, I want to become an interior designer. My hobbies are drawing and designing. I want people to know that I am a girl from Southeast who sees the light in every situation and takes that inspiration and runs with it.

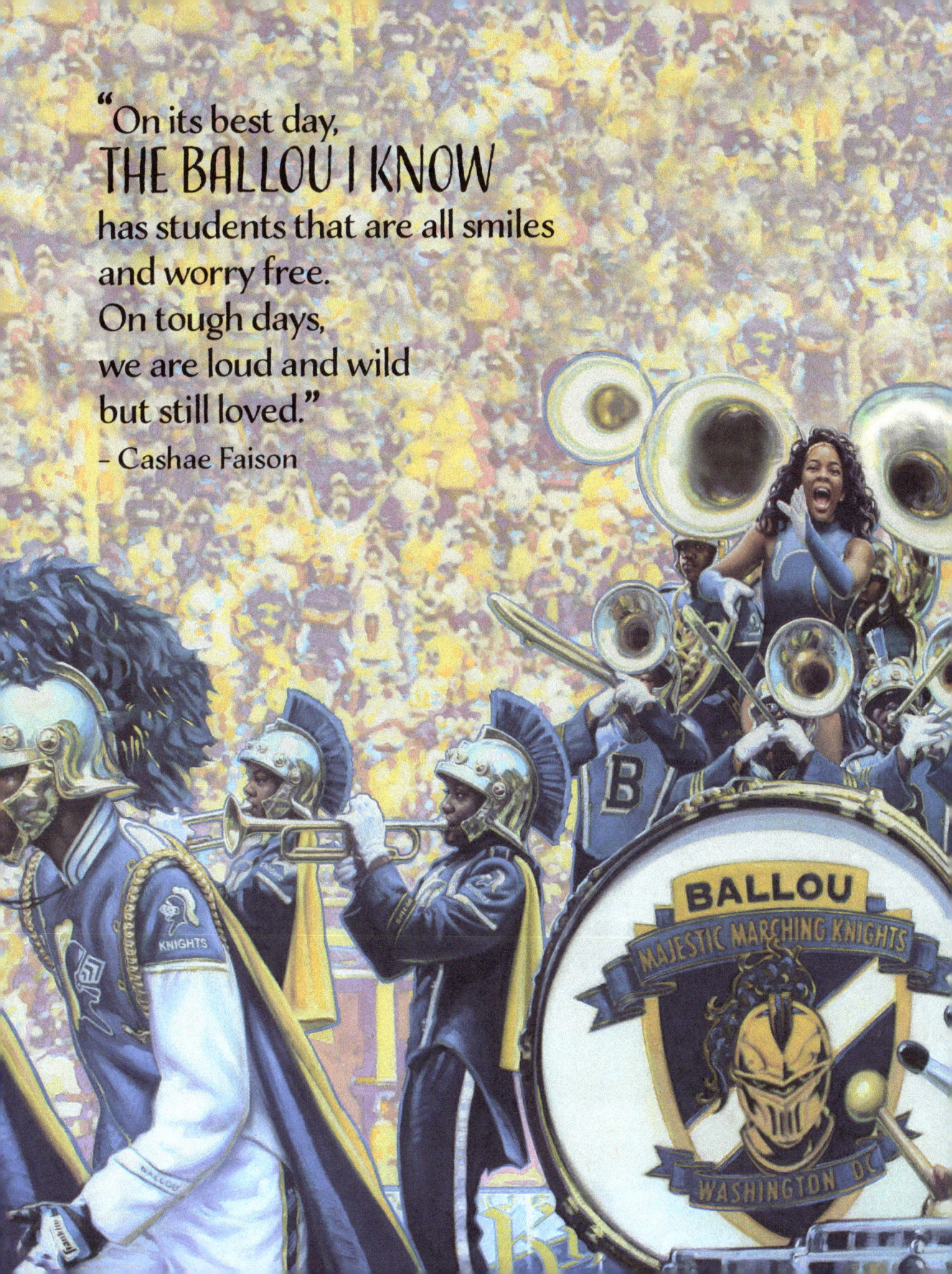

TEXTING OUR TRUTH
Trevaughn Boomer

What You Think

> I hate what they're saying about Ballou!

Well.... I mean, isn't it true?

It's all over the news...

Like nobody from Ballou actually goes to college?

> Maaaaan... u don't know what ur talking about

> Ballou students go to college every year

> And they come back and tell us how it is all the time!!! 😡😡😡

What You Think

Psshhh. That's not what I heard

Ballou kids are lazy...

> Don't believe everything u hear

And y'all got negative vibes

> What? We got good vibes at Ballou!

> It's a big family that supports each other

For what? Ballou students don't have futures...

Screen 1:

> Well, actually. 😣😣😣
>
> Ballou does a lot for our futures.
>
> Like, they have hospitality and culinary arts classes...
>
> and auto tech training...
>
> so students can get great jobs right away.
>
> Or they go to college, like I said.

> But what about all that violence in the community?

> There might be violence, but there's HOPE because of Ballou.

> What do you mean? Kids don't even go to class!

> Well, not any different than the rest of DCPS...
>
> And anyway, u gotta look at the whole picture.
>
> There's lots of reasons for absences at schools like Ballou.

Screen 2:

> Some kids have to work and provide for their families...
>
> Some kids have to look after younger siblings or their own children...
>
> Some kids have unstable living situations...
>
> Sometimes it's hard to still attend school while taking care of everything else

> That's not an excuse...
>
> You can't expect to do well in life if you don't go to school.

> I hear that. But it's the reality here.
>
> And just because kids can't always go to class doesn't mean they can't learn.
>
> There should be lots of chances to catch up. Different schools need different things, right?

> I guess...

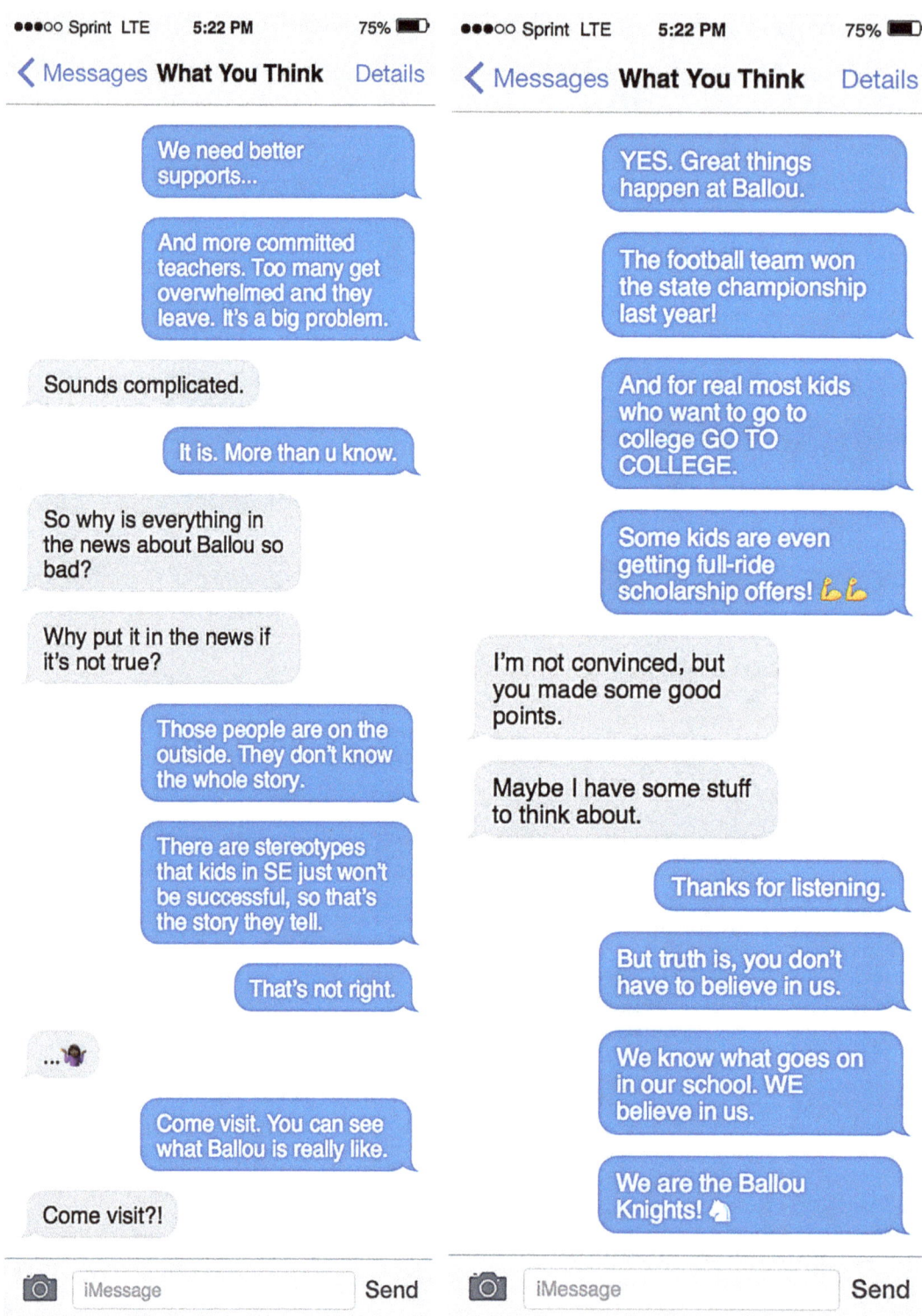

"THERE MIGHT BE VIOLENCE, BUT THERE'S HOPE BECAUSE OF BALLOU."

TREVAUGHN BOOMER

I'm from Southeast DC. In the future, I want to be a successful forensic scientist. I enjoy hanging with my friends, playing sports, and playing games. My hobbies are playing football, going out with friends, and eating. I want people to know that I'm a quiet and hardworking person who loves my family.

"YOU CAN CHANGE YOURSELF FOR WORSE OR FOR GOOD, IF YOU THINK THAT YOU CAN BE BETTER, YOU CAN BE BETTER."

DIG DEEPER
Tyrese Linder

I like to learn.
Not just school learning,
but what's happening in the real world —
philosophy, psychology, determinism.
If you think about free will, some say it's an illusion
Like when you touch a hot stove
And you're like pssssst...
Does your brain move your hand or do you?
If everything is already determined,
it doesn't matter what you do.
But I am determined that that's not true.

You can change yourself for worse or for good.
If you think that you can be better, you can be better.
You can't lie to your mind.

I like history.
There is the history they teach you in school,
but it could be false. It could be brainwashing.
Like how some history books teach us about Africa,
They show us the bad side — huts, mud, and all that.
But if you dig deeper,
You will find out that Africa is not actually like that,
You will find out it's much much more.
They don't tell you that
History is also about the evil of the world.
History changes my mindset.

You can change yourself for worse or for good.
If you think that you can be better, you can be better.
You can't lie to your mind.

You should find the truth for yourself in the world.
Why not?
If you only just hear what other people are saying,
you're never going to hear both sides of the story.
Without both sides, people are like mobs
If you only hear one side, you're just following blindly,
If you just do what you're told, you will never grow as a person.
What do you stand for?
It's easy to dig deeper —
Research
Ask around
Just read
I used to be stubborn, mad, mean
I learned you don't have to be that way.
There's no reason to walk around mad
I just didn't want to do that anymore
I started to read and learn more and think about the other things.
I felt relief and I felt like the world was big
I asked myself who is right?
I keep asking myself who is right?
What I mean by that is….

You can change yourself for worse or for good.
If you think that you can be better, you can be better.
You can't lie to your mind.

TYRESE LINDER

I'm from Southeast DC. In the future, I want to work in the fire department. I enjoy playing instruments, reading, and games. I enjoy anything honestly if it's fun. My hobbies are music, chilling with books, movies, or TV shows. I want people to dig deeper.

"THE BALLOU I KNOW is evolving with talent in the stars that no one recognizes."
- Tatiana Robinson

A SCANDALOUS PERCEPTION
Shawma Brown

This perception that we are a "dumb school" is scandalous.
Every day someone waits for something bad to happen here.
The news stays on standby,
Just waiting like bloodhounds,
Waiting to get the next scoop,
Waiting to broadcast our faults.

Why is it that they only want to exploit the negative?

People don't realize how this perception affects the students.
People don't realize how this perception affects *us*.

Don't they realize that most of us aren't privileged?
Don't they realize that we work hard every day,
Facing our fears of getting shot
Just to come to school and learn?

People don't realize what it's like to live in the hood,
That every day we are fighting not to become another statistic.
People don't realize we are trying,
Trying to fix the lens the world uses to view us,
Trying to stay positive when people only recognize the negative.

It hurts my soul deeply,
All the things that people refuse to see.

There is an untold truth of Ballou.
The story is not one-sided.
The Ballou I know has helped me find my identity.
The Ballou I know has changed me for the better.
It has shown me a new perspective on life.
It has given me my freedom.

"PEOPLE DON'T REALIZE THAT OUR TEACHERS SET THEIR EXPECTATIONS HIGH, SHOOTING FOR THE STARS, PAST THE MOON."

Why don't people see these things?
Why is it they only talk about the bad?

People don't know that Ballou has the best school spirit.
People don't care that the principal instilled pride in Ballou.
People don't understand that the principal believed in us when no one else would.

People don't know that our teachers support their students,
That our teachers are our parents,
That our teachers give tough love.
People don't realize that our teachers set their expectations high,
shooting for the stars, past the moon.

This is the untold truth of Ballou
That people don't understand:
That Ballou is a family,
That Ballou is *my* family.

SHAWMA BROWN

I'm from Washington, DC. I wrote this to express my feelings about Ballou. In the future I want to become a freelance journalist. I enjoy traveling and writing poetry and short stories. I want people to know that I work to make a difference in the world.

COLLEGE-BOUND
Cashae Faison

In February of my junior year, I learned we were going to take a college trip to North Carolina. But only a few people could go. We had to write an essay about why we thought we should go. I wrote about how I deeply wanted to go to college, and especially wanted to leave DC. I wanted to get out of my comfort zone.

When I learned that I was going on the trip, I was excited. I called my mother, my uncles, and my siblings and told them about it. They were excited for me. They knew I was destined to go away to college.

When I think of college, I know that I'm going to learn to be independent. I'll have to work. I'll have to keep up with a car, a schedule for work and class. I'm going to have to make my own money. I have to worry about my own living arrangements. But that doesn't scare me. I'm ready to go. I'm also nervous because I won't know anyone and I don't like big crowds, but I'll get used to it. Another reason I want to go to college is because none of my mother's kids went to college. I'm the youngest of four. It will be a big accomplishment for her, not just for me.

I have three cousins who went to college. Their lives are better because they went. That's what I want. I know when you get a degree more opportunities come your way. I want to make a lot of money so that I can help my family and help other people. When I'm with my mother and we see a homeless person we will often buy them food. My mother taught me to give back to people who are less fortunate and showed the importance of helping people, especially those who don't have money. After I graduate from college, I want to buy my mother a house and a car. I want to pay her back for all the support she gives me. My mother provides for me, and she is there for me always.

When I got off the bus at the first campus on the trip, I saw statues everywhere. There were plants and flowers everywhere, too. I saw the Greek plaques. It was so different from everything I see in DC. Those things aren't in the Southeast area where I live. I also saw students going to class. The students looked happy and they looked like me. It was an HBCU. I know I want to go to an HBCU because you can meet people who have been through the same things as you. I want to be around people who understand my life. We also saw lecture rooms, and they were really big. That made me feel a little anxious about how well I could do. But it also made me excited. I'm excited to try different things.

"I CAN REALLY PICTURE MYSELF AS A COLLEGE STUDENT. AND NEXT YEAR, THAT'LL BE ME."

I know college is the place for me. I'm grateful for the opportunities to visit so I know what it will be like on campus. If I did not get the chance to go, I would have to make the choice just based on what other people say and the internet. I need to see the colleges, talk to people, be there and witness the students' daily routine. I imagine myself having good small classes and great relationships with my professors. I can really picture myself as a college student. And next year, that'll be me.

CASHAE FAISON

I'm from Washington, DC. I wrote this because I wanted to inform people that Ballou isn't a bad school, and they shouldn't make assumptions. In the future, I want to become an entrepreneur and own a clothing store. I enjoy singing, going out with my friends, and spending time with my family. I really want people to know that I am not just a statistic. I'll be more.

IF BALLOU DIDN'T EXIST
Tremayne Gross

Ballou is a community, where teachers have close relationships with you, where even the principal pays attention to you, knows you by name, knows who you are, knows when something's good and when something's wrong.

Ballou is a place where students grow and mature, and attitudes change for the better, where students can become leaders and take responsibility for their actions.

Ballou is a place where we support each other. When you are struggling, there is help, from teachers, and the principal, and each other. We lift each other up.

When I arrived at Ballou, I expected that I'd be by myself, that I'd be quiet and wouldn't talk to anyone, that I wouldn't open up, that I'd be shy.

That's who I was then. I just didn't talk to a lot of people. I'd just do my work and then leave, without interacting much. I was satisfied with not talking. I didn't really know those other people. It was easier not to, easier to just stay by myself.

In the ninth grade I was short — 4'11". I was chubby. The other students at Ballou didn't even think that I went there because I looked so much younger. They thought I was somebody's kid. I looked like a child. I was the shortest person at school. I wanted to be taller. I thought about it day and night. I wanted to fit in, but didn't feel like I did. So I would just do my work and go home. And because all I did was work, I had a 3.9 GPA and was in top the 10 of my class — the only boy in the top 10.

But it wasn't enough. I had always wanted to play football. I tried out, and got on the team. After that, I started talking to everybody — people on the team, other kids in school, teachers. I just started talking. Football got me out of my shell. I wasn't by myself anymore. I was part of a team, part of a family, part of a community. I felt comfortable. I made friends, and they had my back. We helped each other.

And it wasn't just football. My teachers, the principal, even the guidance counselor — they were all very helpful, too. They were always giving me advice, checking up on me, and watching my grades.

If Ballou didn't exist, none of these things may have happened. I don't know who I'd be now. But I know this — I'm not that quiet, chubby, 4'11" kid anymore. I'm more confident, more mature, a team player. I'm social. I'm a good student.

Today, I'm thinking about college — and when I get there, I'm not worried about fitting in.

"BALLOU IS A PLACE WHERE WE SUPPORT EACH OTHER. WHEN YOU ARE STRUGGLING, THERE IS HELP... WE LIFT EACH OTHER UP."

TREMAYNE GROSS

I'm from Washington, DC. I wrote this to show how I've changed over the years. In the future, I want to be a business owner, and I plan on going to a four-year college. I enjoy listening to music, and my hobbies are sports, gaming systems, and going out. I want people to know that I'm an outgoing, nice, and determined person. I'm always chilling.

TIP SHEET

My advice to the 4'11", chubby, quiet kid just coming to Ballou...

- There's a lot of support here. Take advantage of that.

- Don't be afraid to open up, to get close to people, even if you're shy.

- Choose your friends and your activities wisely.

- You need to graduate. Pay attention to what you need to do to make that happen.

- Skipping school and getting in trouble is foolish. Don't be a fool.

- Be your own unique self. You're special in your own way, even if you don't know it, or don't like it. Yet.

- Believe in yourself.

THE BALLOU I KNOW
Darmeisha Moore

DARMEISHA MOORE

I am from Washington, DC. I like to sleep, cook, work, and hang out with my friends. I want to run my own business or be a social worker so that I can help other people out. I wanted to be part of the book so I could tell people about Ballou and where we come from. I hope that readers will get a better sense of the students here and see that we're not all bad. We are more than what people make us out to be.

THE BALLOU I KNOW

is ambitious,
and nothing is impossible
It is all about helping all students find their place
It is a family and a place to call home
On its best day,
the Ballou I know is motivating, and we sparkle
On a tough day, it's a struggle
You might not know it from the outside looking in,
Or from looking away,
Or from not looking at all,
But the Ballou I Know is…

We face everything and rise.

LOOKING UP
Davia Cain

I used to get bullied in elementary school. I was tall. I was taller than all of my classmates, both the boys and the girls. The bullying wasn't physical, but it still hurt. They talked about me behind my back. They called me names that I did not like. They called me giraffe. I really didn't pay attention because I knew if I showed my feelings they probably would have bullied me physically. But I was never the child to let that happen.

I have always been a confident and outspoken person. Even when people had negative effects on me, I saw the positive side. For example, since I was tall, I would always get picked first on the team. I had opportunities to play around the country with AAU. Playing basketball and volleyball made me feel healthy and athletic. I was always playing sports, and that's where my confidence came from. When I started getting all the rebounds and and-one's, people stopped calling me names, and instead they cheered me on.

I've always been confident in school as well. To be a student athlete you have to have a good GPA. I've been making honor roll since ninth grade. It's important for me to work hard in school so that recruiters can reward me with a full-ride scholarship. It's never been hard for me to be focused on schoolwork because I am very hard on myself and competitive. In sports, you have to push yourself to go hard in order to win the championship. In school, that championship is making honor roll. Both things make me feel happy about the person I am today.

One other thing that makes me proud? I have won homecoming every year since middle school. To some people running for homecoming is hard because people in the school have to vote for you. So that means you have to think about your haters and how many friends you have. I've always been the type that people were cool with, so that's not a problem. And now no one bullies me for my height. Instead people wish they were tall and slim, too, so they (literally!) look up to me.

I experienced a lot during my childhood. I learned not to let the past affect your future, and to pursue who you want to be and what you want to do in life. I learned to worry about loving yourself instead of loving the idea of other people loving you. I never thought that I would block the negativity from my life, but I learned that when you block hatred and bad things, a lot of opportunities will come your way.

"I LEARNED TO WORRY ABOUT LOVING YOURSELF INSTEAD OF LOVING THE IDEA OF OTHER PEOPLE LOVING YOU."

DAVIA CAIN

I'm from Southeast Washington, DC. I wrote this because I wanted to let people know that everybody goes through stuff and you're not alone. In the future I want to attend college playing varsity volleyball. My hobbies are playing sports: basketball, volleyball, softball, and flag-football. I want people to know that I love playing sports and learning and experiencing new things.

Ballou High School report: Teachers were pressured to pass students

pressured   requirements

extreme number of absences,

failures at many levels

diploma

graduation

Principal Yetunde Reeves
termination   replace

Students need to be in school for each class.   taking care of younger siblings, transportation.

other high schools

not the first time

A RESPONSE FROM TRUTH
Amya McKoy

*In this unique take on Blackout Poetry, the author blacked-out the parts of the article that she felt were inaccurate, leaving only a few words and phrases of truth. She then used those remaining words (in bold) to draft this response letter to decision makers.

Dear DCPS, Decision Makers, The Bureaucracy, All of You,

So, my school has been under fire, and I take personal offense. I don't appreciate my intelligence being doubted. Sometimes I doubt whether the people in charge have the requirements to be where they are.

Now more than ever, students are pressured to be successful. To go to college. To get scholarships. You are so quick to call us troubled kids, to talk about the problems you think we have, but you ignore the real ones like teachers with an extreme number of absences. Those problems are ignored.

I'm sorry, but you've had failures at many levels. From not being able to connect with the students you work with, to making them doubt their education and school. We want to walk across the stage and grab our diploma and brag about our wonderful graduation. But instead we grieve the loss of Principal Yetunde Reeves, for her termination. I call for *you* to be replaced with people who know how to listen to a student's needs.

Also, I'm sorry that we have lives outside of school and have to spend time taking care of younger siblings, and that transportation can be a challenge because the bus never comes on time. I'm sorry it's a little hard to adhere to your views of the perfect student because, as you say, students need to be in school for every class.

I'm sorry that Ballou isn't like other high schools; we are stronger and a little more resilient.

Sincerely,
Amya McKoy

P.S. This is not the first time you've failed to understand what your students need, although it could be the last if you took the time to understand them.

Author's Note: This letter was written in the midst of the controversy. Even though this is no longer an immediate and burning issue, some of the same mistakes are still being made. I fear that DCPS is still making decisions that are not addressing student needs, and still focusing on the wrong things. What happened to us last year is another example of how DCPS is not always in touch with the people that they are supposed to be serving. This letter is an artifact from that impact.

"THIS IS NOT THE FIRST TIME YOU'VE FAILED TO UNDERSTAND WHAT YOUR STUDENTS NEED, ALTHOUGH IT COULD BE THE LAST IF YOU TOOK THE TIME TO UNDERSTAND THEM."

AMYA MCKOY

I'm from Southeast DC. I wrote this piece because I saw articles that didn't represent my school and I wanted to tell some truths. I'm in the Ballou band and I like to read and write. In the future, I want to be an author.

"On its best day, THE BALLOU I KNOW is fun and challenging. On its tough days, it's where we make our own glue from scum to stick together."

– Tatiana Robinson

THE BALLOU I KNOW
Christopher Holbrook

The Ballou I know is a place where
we come together as one,
put our differences aside and face adversity.
The Ballou I know is a place where
the mission is a dream
to seek a better future.

They ask,
Why is it when I look in your face
I see dark within your eyes as if
you stare out in space?
My only response: I don't want to be late,
got to change my own ways to create a better state.

The Ballou I know helps you understand
it all starts in your mind, even though society
makes you feel like it's a crime to keep trying.
But in Ballou it gets deeper. See.

The Ballou I know sheds light on the dark,
makes glow from the growth,
until you feel that inner spark.

The Ballou I know makes you want to get better.
It's never the end of the story,
but it's the beginning of the letter.

They ask,
Why do you push through and persevere?
I respond saying, Have you ever cried a bunch of tears?
It's a lot of pain from shame, especially
with pointing fingers and taking the blame.
But the Ballou I know
allows you the opportunity
to change the game.

> "IT ALL STARTS
> IN YOUR MIND,
> EVEN THOUGH SOCIETY
> MAKES YOU FEEL LIKE
> IT'S A CRIME
> TO KEEP TRYING."

CHRISTOPHER HOLBROOK

I'm from Southeast Washington, DC. I wrote this poem because I wanted the youth, including whoever may read it, to understand they're never alone. I enjoy playing football and running track because it shows some of my unique abilities. My hobbies are studying, singing, and playing sports. I want people to know that I was one of those people witnessing gunshots and bullets flying, I know what it's like to be in a falling household, but that doesn't define me. I live with a purpose. Langston Hughes once said "To be black is to be in a constant state of rage." Don't ever let that point be proven, use that rage as motivation to make beneficial changes and live your best life.

LET'S BE REAL
Shae'Lynn Ames

[Scene: It's a sunny evening at the Lincoln Memorial. Thousands are gathered. Shae' Lynn, a twelfth-grade student from Ballou Senior High School, steps up to the podium.]

Good Evening Ladies and Gentlemen,

[Crowd responds with "Good Evening."]

We're gathered here today, in honor of Truth and Reality. We must know that there's not one without the other. We must remember and acknowledge their value. When stories go untold, the world is left in a dilemma, as Truth and Reality get separated. It's our job as the people to unite them. It's my job to express why.

Truth holds us accountable. Reality keeps us grounded. Recently, both have been tarnished. In many ways, society is to blame, in that society demands and enforces a change of Truth, in order to meet its own expectations. This change of Truth affects Reality.

Society pounds on those who they see as weak. They make them targets. They believe in only what they want for themselves. We must watch out. Society attacks by making us indifferent to Truth and Reality. Society separates them as if they have no purpose, but together they should serve the purpose of guidance. They guide us to independence, they guide us through our sorrows, they guide us through our defeat. They help us overcome.

For example, the Truth about my school — or at least the Truth that society has made — isn't our Reality. We worked our butts off to change the narrative, but that's being blindsided. Wiped out. Now I think it's time to make society listen. They must change the way they view our Reality, and we must all keep the real Truth in our minds. (Pause.)

It's our time to change the narrative. It's time to seek the things we deserve: dignity, respect, adventure, and life. (Says slowly.) It's time for us, the people, to be the change. We must reconnect Truth and Reality. We must hold society accountable, and prove them wrong.

[Crowd cheers loudly.]

Although life deals with right and wrong, that's not what life is ABOUT. Life is about experiences and what you make of them. Life is about making mistakes and learning from them. Every day is a lesson. Every day is a gift. And every day is a chance to make it right. This is OUR chance to make things right.

(With passion) Together we are the change! We know our Truth! Will society make the change for us?

[Crowd yells, "NO!"]

So we'll step up and lead.
Now Let's Be Real!

> "IT'S OUR TIME
> TO CHANGE THE NARRATIVE.
> IT'S TIME TO SEEK
> THE THINGS WE DESERVE:
> DIGNITY, RESPECT,
> ADVENTURE, AND LIFE."

SHAE'LYNN AMES

I'm from Southeast DC. I wrote this because I wanted to express my views and be heard. In the future I want to be a physical therapist. I enjoy listening to music and helping others. My hobbies are dancing and writing. I really want people to know that I am a straight-A student. Also I have ten siblings!

THE BALLOU I KNOW
Raven Brown

You think Ballou is rowdy. It can be, at lunch,
but the Ballou I know is also quiet -
in the classroom where thinking and learning are happening every day.

You think Ballou is violent. It can be — there used to be fights almost every day.
But as students mature, there's less of that.
And more modeling for younger kids.

You think there's no learning here.
But in the Ballou I know, we have study hall every day after school.
We study math and English, yes.
But we're also mentored to grow as people, emotionally.
We are taught tools for coping, patience, and discipline.

You think there are shootings at Ballou.
Did you hear that on the news?
There are no shootings at school, not at the Ballou I know.
But it can be a violent neighborhood, outside of school,
outside of the Ballou I know.

You think Ballou students are disrespectful and lack self control.
But it actually takes extra control and discipline
to not get mixed up in the violence of the neighborhood.

You think we're lazy.
But we take AP and Honors classes.
We sometimes have three assignments due the same day,
and we participate in sports and cheerleading,
while keeping our grades up.
I don't feel lazy.

You think we're dropouts, we're failing,
we can't read or write or comprehend.
You think we're on drugs, going nowhere.
But in the Ballou I know, we get accepted to summer programs.
We earn scholarships to take college-level classes
at Harvard and Duke and others.

"IF YOU THINK THE TEACHERS DON'T CARE, YOU DON'T KNOW THE TEACHERS HERE. YOU DON'T KNOW THE BALLOU I KNOW."

You think no parenting takes place here.
But there's a lot of parenting.
There are a lot of people who are loving, who discipline me,
who are helpful and encouraging, who sacrifice for my success,
who are hard-working even though there are no jobs.

You think the teachers don't care, don't track attendance, look the other way,
But at the Ballou I know, teachers do care.
Teachers like Ms. Yates and Ms. Ingram don't look the other way.
They're always there, always supportive,
always pushing us in the best way, in a way that helps us grow.
If you think the teachers don't care, you don't know the teachers here.

You don't know the Ballou I know.

RAVEN BROWN

I'm from Washington, DC. I wrote this because I wanted to tell my story about Ballou. In the future, I want to give advice to the young Ballou students. I enjoy music, and my hobbies are cheerleading, shopping, dancing, and listening to music. I want people to know that I'm chill.

THE LOVE INSIDE
Milan Womack

I feel safer inside Ballou than outside. The school is surrounded by different hoods, and Southeast can get real crazy when the sun drops. It's a lot of killing. There's a lot of violence. When the sun drops, that's when most of the bad in Southeast comes out, like drug dealers, killers, robbers. Young kids doing crazy stuff. You can be leaving an afterschool activity and just run into gun violence. Seeing someone get shot for no good reason, it puts you in the mindset of:

'That could have been me.'
'What if I'm next?'
'What if I get caught in the crossfire?'

It's something traumatizing for someone so young who's trying to do good, who has a promising future.

So this is the environment a lot of Ballou students live in, and where I grew up. When I came to Ballou, I wasn't an outstanding student. And I wasn't very into my academics. I was more interested in being out around my hood. I can't talk about what I was doing. I'm not proud of it. But being at Ballou, and having the relationship I have with my teachers, changed my thoughts about what being a young African-American male is, about not being another statistic to my environment.

My ninth grade year, I wasn't really into school. So I came with the intention to show face and

> "IT'S EASY TO GIVE UP. BUT IT TAKES A STRONG MAN TO WORK THROUGH CHALLENGES."

to leave. It came to a point when one day I was like, "School is not for me. I'm about to drop out and be full-time out and about." But one teacher helped me see the bigger picture. Me and my math teacher built a relationship together. I'm a math person. I'm a numbers person. So I always went to her class. And one day she pulled me aside because she noticed my attendance. I wasn't going to other classes, only her class. The other classes, I was skipping. She told me, "I've seen your attendance. How can you be here but not the other classes? You need those classes to be successful and to graduate." But I didn't really like the rest of my classes. I'm not an English person. So at first I wasn't listening. And after we had the conversation, she said, "Let me tell you something: It's easy to give up, but it takes a strong man to work through challenges."

At the time I didn't really listen to her. I was going through a hard time mentally and emotionally, having to deal with some legal trouble. This caused severe stress between my parents and me, which ultimately led me into the streets, staying out late nights and being up to no good. But I did keep going to school. It took me a little while to start really going to classes and to be there, mentally and physically. But once I started going, I started finding the joy in the better things and in going to school. It felt good being able to read and not be discouraged. I was proud of being able to announce myself and announce my answers. It felt good to say it properly, to say it right.

So I continued to come to school and I continued to put in my best effort. And Ballou helped me to step up and become the bigger person that I aspired to be.

As a junior, I had the chance to speak before City Council about what Ballou means to me. I proudly told them the story of my transformation. I told them:

"I came to the conclusion that I know I can do better, and I have to do better. So I began to get serious about my work. I started to raise my grades, and now in my junior year I am an honor roll student not accepting or settling for anything other than a B to an A+. This is an extreme accomplishment and honor to me and my family, and it may not have happened if I were not blessed to be at Ballou with teachers, mentors, and a principal who have truly impacted my life, inside and outside of the classroom."

It was important for me to speak that day because I felt like it was my duty as a Knight to let the council members know about the great encouragement and teaching that Ballou offers in the school. The teachers, counselors, and principal really make an impact on the students who come into Ballou with a bad mindset, not wanting to be in school. There are many students like me at Ballou. We want to break that cycle for us and our future kids. And for kids who are younger than us so they can see how much better life can be, without being another drug dealer, another killer, another shooter. To be educated instead of being blinded to the real world. It's more to life than running around your hood, claiming your hood. You can claim your hood every day, but the hood don't love you.

Instead, your teachers love you. The staff members in the building love you. Your fellow students love you. And most importantly, Ballou as a whole loves you. And their love builds a love inside you so you can love yourself.

MILAN WOMACK

I'm from Southeast DC. I wrote this because I wanted people to read my side of the story about Ballou. In the future, I want to be able to come back and see how the book affected young people's lives. I enjoy seeing positivity in my city. My hobbies are football and gaming. I want people to know that I come from the struggle.

"THE BALLOU I KNOW has students. It has teachers. It has celebrations. It has love. It has hate and it has homework. It has hard, hard work."

– Amya McKoy

AFTERWORD

The Ballou I know is filled with powerful students who come from different backgrounds with different experiences and different stories. The Ballou I know is filled with strength, courage, and resilience.

The past four years have been a journey. A journey that has been EVERYTHING; a journey that I am blessed, proud, honored, grateful, and ecstatic to be a part of. It is my prayer that as you read this amazing collection, that you became a part of the journey, too.

The last four years have entailed challenges and triumphs, obstacles and victories, but most importantly, growth and reflection. I have watched these amazing young kings and queens grow — grow from children to young adults, grow from the voiceless to the voice of reason, and grow into authors who have decided to write their own narrative, to tell their own story. Hopefully these phenomenal young people have taken you on a journey that provides insight into their growth, their process, their story. Hopefully their stories empower, enlighten, inspire, and motivate you.

The Ballou we know is a community, a family, and a bond that is unbreakable. The Ballou we know is filled with boldness, courage, creativity, ambition, uniqueness, and determination. Many people think they know what goes on at Ballou High School, but until you walk in the building and get a glimpse of what we have to offer, you'll truly never know the Ballou we know.

To my 2K19 children, the journey of high school is coming to an end and the journey of life-after-high school will soon begin. Now it is time for you to continue your process of growth. As you do, remember everything that being a Knight entails; remember everything that being a member of 2K19 means. Remember every lesson that every person in the building taught you; remember every person who cares, every teacher, administrator, principal, dean, social worker, school counselor, librarian, mentor, program, or friend. Remember your Ballou family; remember we are Knights!!! We are BIG BAD BALLOU!!!

Always know that no matter what, there is nothing you can do that will ever make me stop loving you. Create your own story; write your own narrative. As you leave behind this chapter of your life and begin a new chapter, always remember that the only person you are accountable for is you, and the only person that can tell your story is you...create your story and live your dreams!

The journey continues....

— Ms. Nakisha Yates
Ballou High School Teacher

ACKNOWLEDGMENTS

This fourth volume of the Ballou Story Project could not have been possible without the support of a number of hard-working folks who believed in the importance of empowering these young people to share their stories.

For inviting us into their classrooms and coordinating these writers, we cannot thank enough Ballou teachers Nakisha Yates and Tierra Ingram. These educators knew that providing their students the opportunity to speak their truths was important for their growth, their self-perception, and their dignity. We are grateful for the time and support they gave in making this project possible. Most of all, we are grateful for the tough love they dole out to young people every day.

For mentoring these writers throughout the process we thank Story Coaches Holly Bass, Stacey Picard, Sarai Johnson, and Barrett Smith. It was Stacey's poignant exercise that gave rise to the recurring refrain of this book, and that gave this book its shape. She and fellow Story Coaches gave generously of their time and their talents, as well as their hearts. We are lucky to count them as members of this team!

For the striking photography throughout this book we thank a team of Ballou student photographers led by Shout Mouse Photo Coach and Shootback founder Lana Wong. During multiple photo shoot days, Lana helped students capture powerful imagery of each other and of their school by providing both cameras and mentorship. Student photography forms the backbone of this book. We thank all of these photographers for their insight, and their vision.

For the smart graphic design of this book — and for all around awesomeness — we thank Barrett Smith, who invested countless hours in making sure these stories and images did these students justice. Her dedication helped these voices get the respect and consideration they deserve, and we are grateful.

None of this work would have been possible without a generous grant from the Sylarn Foundation, for which we are enormously grateful. The folks behind this fund introduced us to Ballou and served as constant encouragement and support.

And most of all we thank these writers: Tati, Amya, Raven, Jada, Tremayne, Aniyah, Gabe, Shae'Lynn, Shaheed, Cashae, Me'Chelle, Trevaughn, Shawma, Andrenae, Davia, Chris, Ahmaiya, Milan, Syamyia, Darmeisha, and Tyrese. We thank them for advocating for themselves and their school, and for initiating this book. These passionate, thoughtful, dedicated students — who often gave up lunch periods to write — were driven by their conviction that their voices and their stories matter. The courage of these authors will stay with us. Writing with—and learning from—these incredible teens was such a gift, and a joy.

— Kathy Crutcher
Founder, Shout Mouse Press

ABOUT SHOUT MOUSE PRESS

Shout Mouse Press is a nonprofit writing and publishing program dedicated to amplifying unheard voices.

Through writing workshops designed for all levels of literacy, Shout Mouse empowers writers from marginalized communities to tell their own stories in their own voices and — as published authors — to act as agents of change.

Our authors include incarcerated, immigrant, minority, and otherwise marginalized teens, all of whom are served by mission-aligned partner organizations working to provide enrichment and leadership opportunities for their communities.

Shout Mouse authors have produced original children's books, comics, novels, and memoir and poetry collections that engage a diverse audience as well as open hearts and minds.

You can find our full catalog of #OwnVoices mission-driven books at: shoutmousepress.org/catalog.

ABOUT SHOOTBACK

Shootback empowers young people to tell their own stories and express their creative voices through photography, writing, and critical thinking about the world around them. Shootback started in Nairobi, Kenya in 1997 by putting cameras in the hands of teens from Mathare, one of Africa's largest slums, and culminated in the publication of Shootback: Photos by Kids from the Nairobi Slums, a documentary film, and an international traveling exhibition. Twenty+ years on, Shootback continues to train a new generation of young photographers in Nairobi and DC in collaboration with various nonprofit organizations.

Shout Mouse Press is proud to partner with the Shootback team, who coach our authors to produce striking original photography for our books.

You can find out more about their work at: shootbackproject.org

SHOUT MOUSE PRESS TEEN/YA TITLES:

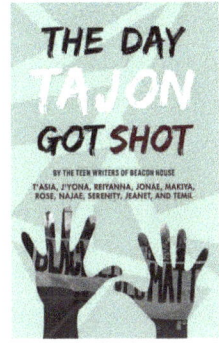 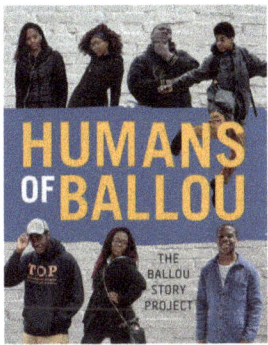 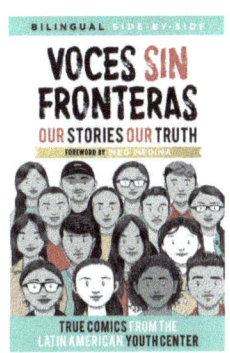 

Voces Sin Fronteras
Latin American Youth Center (2018)
A collection of graphic memoirs written by immigrant youth.

The Day Tajon Got Shot
Beacon House (2017)
Teen authors explore a police shooting from multiple perspectives.

How to Grow Up Like Me
Our Lives Matter
Humans of Ballou
Ballou Story Project (2014-2016)
Students from Ballou High School speak for themselves through photos and essays.

The Untold Story of The Real Me: Young Voices From Prison
Free Minds Book Club (2016)
A collection of poetry by incarcerated young writers.

And more!

For the full catalog of Shout Mouse books, including illustrated children's books, visit **shoutmousepress.org**. Books are also available through Amazon, select bookstores, and select distributors, including Ingram and Follett. For bulk orders, educator inquiries, and nonprofit discounts contact **orders@shoutmousepress.org**.

www.ingramcontent.com/pod-product-compliance
Lightning Source LLC
Chambersburg PA
CBHW051349110526
44591CB00025B/2951